TASTE THE WORLD!

CORN

WORLD BOOK

www.worldbook.com

TABLE OF CONTENTS

BEFORE YOU BEGIN

Included in this book are a few recipes that allow you to "taste the world!" Before you begin, look on page 46 for some helpful hints. Read the recipes carefully and always ask an adult to help—especially when handling knives or using the stove. Besides, cooking is easier and more fun when you work together!

As we travel around the world, we'll explore my history, discover some fun facts, and learn to prepare some delicious recipes. Along the way, you may read words that are new to you. If I can explain what a word means easily, I'll do it right where you are reading. If I use the word many times, or if the explanation is complicated, I will put the word in **boldface** (type that **looks like this**). Boldface words are defined in a glossary in the back of the book.

WHAT IS CORN?

Corn is a cereal grass distantly related to wheat, rice, oats, and barley. Corn is called maize outside the United States.

Maize is a Native American word that means "sacred mother" or "giver of life." Native Americans living in what is now Mexico learned how to grow corn thousands of years ago. That's how corn came to be called Indian corn. But today the term *Indian corn* generally refers only to varieties of corn that produce ears with multicolored kernels.

THERE'S GOLD IN THESE FIELDS!

Corn is sometimes called "prairie gold" because farmers in the prairie states of the United States earn money from the corn they grow. The prairie region extends from central Texas up through parts of Montana and North Dakota.

VEGGIE OR GRAIN?

When sweet corn is harvested before it is fully grown, it is usually considered a vegetable. That is, it is grown to be eaten fresh. If corn is dried and used for livestock feed or grinding into meal and flour, it is a grain. But technically, corn is a grain because it comes from a type of grass.

Corn and corn meal are important foods for people in many parts of the world. Corn meal is made by grinding up dried corn. In the United States, corn meal can be used to make such foods as **grits,** cornbread, muffins, and **hush-puppies.** In Mexico, corn meal is used to make a thin, round flatbread called **tortilla** and a thick porridge called **polenta.**

DID YOU KNOW that there are thousands of varieties (kinds) of corn? During our journey, however, we will explore only the six major kinds of corn: dent, flint, flour, sweet, popcorn, and waxy corn.

A CLOSER LOOK AT THE CORN PLANT. . .

Corn plants begin life as a seed. The seed consists of the *embryo*, the *endosperm*, and the *seed coat*. The embryo is the part of the seed that develops into a new plant. The endosperm contains mostly soft starch. It stores food energy, which the young corn plant uses in its early development. The seed coat is the thin, tough outer covering that protects the endosperm and embryo from damage.

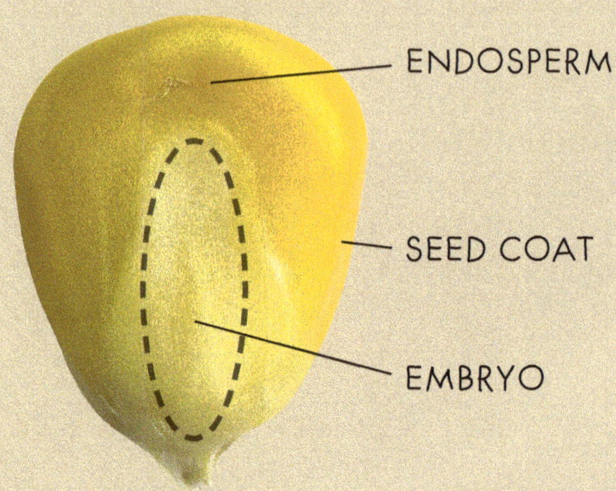

Depending on the type, corn can be grown in most *temperate* (mild) and tropical regions of the world. It grows best in a climate that has warm weather and long, sunny summers. Most types of corn have a growing season of four to six months, usually beginning in April or early May.

The average corn plant grows about 8 to 10 feet (2.5 to 3 meters) tall. But some varieties may grow to only 3 feet (0.9 meter) tall or as tall as 20 feet (6 meters). It takes 60 to 100 days for corn to reach the stage where it's ready for harvesting.

A mature (fully grown) corn plant has roots, a stalk, leaves, and flowering parts. The flowering parts at the top of the stalk are called the *tassel*. The *ear* grows in the middle of the *stalk* (stem). It consists of a hard center called a *cob* that is covered by rows of corn kernels. The ear is tightly wrapped in special leaves called *husks*. A stalk of corn may have one or several ears. Each ear of corn has long soft threads at the top called *silk*.

TASSEL
SILK
EAR
COB
HUSKS
STALK
ROOTS
ODDS OR EVENS?
Every ear of corn has an even number of rows of kernels.
Count 'em!

IN THE BEGINNING...

Scientists have determined that corn developed from a wild tall grass called **teosinte** thousands of years ago in Mexico.

Teosinte still grows wild in parts of Mexico's western Sierra Madre. But the ear of the teosinte plant is very different from today's ear of corn. Teosinte grows a small cob with about 5 to 10 hard kernels. In comparison, modern corn produces a much larger cob with hundreds of soft kernels.

This coin—a United States quarter—shows how small a teosinte ear looked compared to an ear of modern corn.

Corn eventually spread throughout North and South America, where Native Americans grew it as an important food crop. It was most widely grown by the Aztec, the Maya, and the Inca. As the civilizations spread, so did corn. By the late 1400's, Native Americans were growing corn as far away as Argentina, Chile, and Canada.

HOLY CORN!

Many of the people of ancient Mexico, including the Maya and the Aztec, worshiped a corn god.

A sculpture of the Maya corn god. The god's headdress is carved in the shape of ears of corn.

THAT'S SO OLD!

The oldest known corncobs are more than 6,000 years old!

MEXICO

Mayan women prepared corn in many different ways for their families to eat. They made a tasty food by filling corn dough with meat. Today, we call this basic food **tamale.**

SWEET DRINK!

The Maya also used corn to make a fermented drink called **balché.** They sweetened it with honey and spiced it with bark from the balché tree.

Which one? I can't decide!

The Maya and Aztec considered tamales sacred food. They also made thin, corn flatbread, which today is called **tortilla.** Tortillas were first made thousands of years ago. Tortillas were a staple in the diet of the Aztec.

Corn remains a key ingredient in nearly every dish in Mexico today. Tortillas are the country's most popular food. People eat corn tortillas with different foods almost every day. Tortillas are served in or with such delicious foods as **atole, burritos, enchiladas, quesadillas, pozole, tacos, tostadas,** and many other dishes.

Tortillas are not just a staple food in Mexico. Tortillas are also an important food for people in Guatemala, Honduras, Nicaragua, and parts of Costa Rica.

Tortillas have become increasingly popular throughout the world. In the United States, many Americans eat tortillas. They are a popular menu option in many restaurants, from fast food tacos to gourmet dishes.

CORN TORTILLAS

Serves about 7

INGREDIENTS

1 ¾ cups **masa harina** (dry corn flour)   1 ⅛ cups water

STEPS

1. Mix masa harina and hot water together in a medium bowl. Stir until thoroughly mixed. Place dough on a clean, dry surface and press and squeeze with your hands until it's flexible and smooth. If the dough is too sticky, add more masa harina; add water, if it begins to dry out. Cover the dough with plastic wrap or foil and allow to stand for 30 minutes.
2. Preheat a skillet or griddle to medium-high heat.
3. Separate dough into 15 balls, all about the same size. Using your hands or a rolling pin, press each ball of dough between two sheets of plastic wrap until they are flat.
4. Place a single tortilla immediately in the preheated skillet or griddle. Cook it for about 30 seconds, or until it is browned and slightly puffy. Turn the tortilla over and cook the other side for about 30 seconds until it is browned also. Remove from skillet and place it on a plate. Repeat this step with each ball of dough until you have cooked all 15 balls. Cover the tortillas with a towel to keep them warm and moist until ready to serve.

HEADING NORTH NOW TO THE

UNITED STATES

The United States is the world's leading producer and exporter of corn. Native Americans grew corn for thousands of years before the English colonists arrived in North America. They introduced corn to the colonists and taught them how to plant and grow corn and how to make different dishes from corn. Such dishes included cornbread, fried corn cakes, corn soup, and corn pudding. The colonists ate corn at the very first Thanksgiving feast in 1621, at Plymouth Colony in what is now Massachusetts. They invited the Native Americans to be their guests.

DID YOU KNOW that in 1613, English colonists kidnapped Pocahontas, the daughter of a powerful Native American chief. They demanded a boatload of corn as ransom for her return!

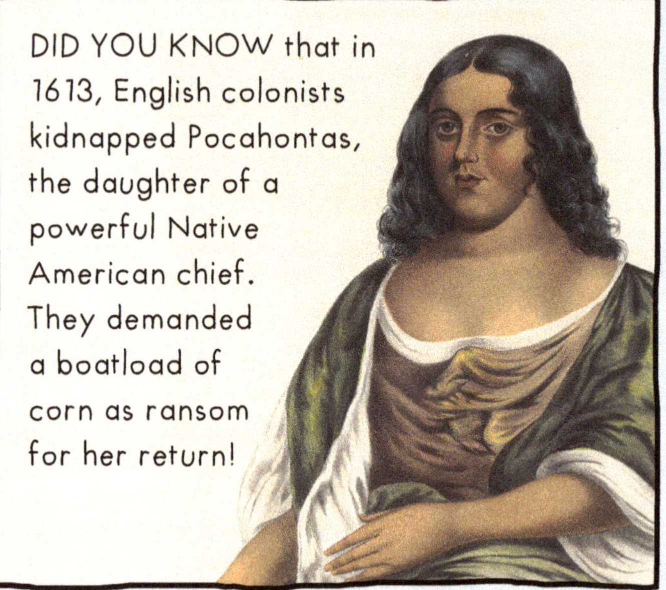

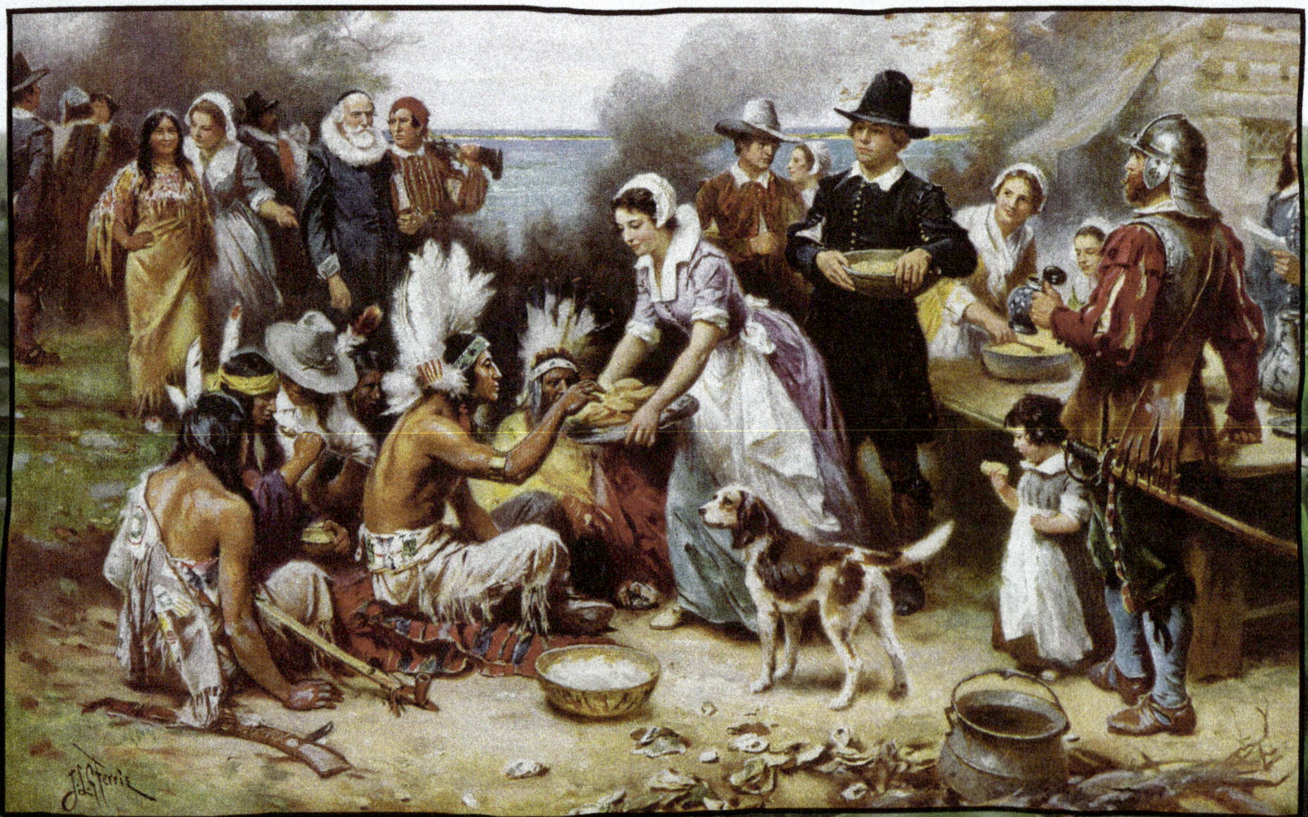

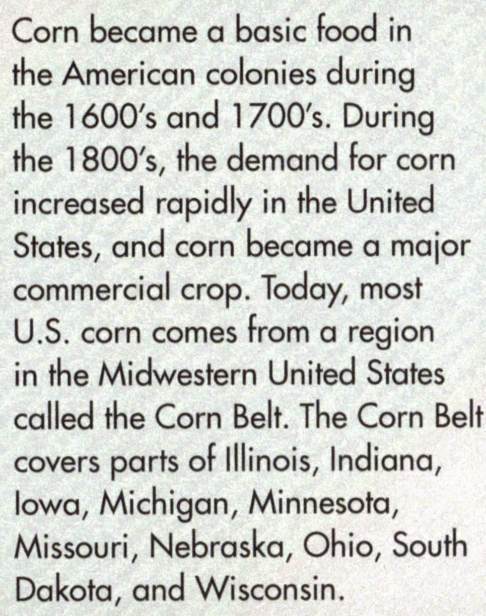

Corn became a basic food in the American colonies during the 1600's and 1700's. During the 1800's, the demand for corn increased rapidly in the United States, and corn became a major commercial crop. Today, most U.S. corn comes from a region in the Midwestern United States called the Corn Belt. The Corn Belt covers parts of Illinois, Indiana, Iowa, Michigan, Minnesota, Missouri, Nebraska, Ohio, South Dakota, and Wisconsin.

LET'S DO SOME CORN MATH!

One hundred bushels, or 800 gallons, of corn can produce about 7,280,000 kernels of corn!

MONEY!

The early American colonists considered corn so valuable that they used it as money to trade for such other items as meat and fur.

DID YOU KNOW that National Maize Day is celebrated annually on the day after Thanksgiving Day in the United States? Maize Day is a day for Americans to celebrate corn's role in the country's different cultures.

Corn syrup is a type of sweetener that is made from the starch in corn.

It is widely used in soft drinks, fruit juices, and even ketchup.

Corn is everywhere! Almost every food Americans eat today contains corn. For example, corn fillers are used in such fast foods as taco meat, hamburger patties, chicken nuggets, and many other foods sold in fast food restaurants. Most French fries are cooked in oil that has corn in it. Many everyday foods, such as soup, pudding, yogurt, mayonnaise, and gravy, contain corn.

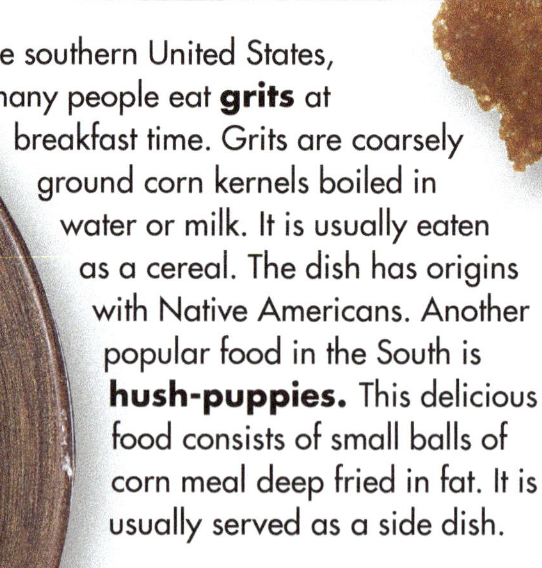

In the southern United States, many people eat **grits** at breakfast time. Grits are coarsely ground corn kernels boiled in water or milk. It is usually eaten as a cereal. The dish has origins with Native Americans. Another popular food in the South is **hush-puppies.** This delicious food consists of small balls of corn meal deep fried in fat. It is usually served as a side dish.

ELOTE: A STREET FOOD

Elote is a Mexican "street food" that is popular both in Mexico and in the United States. Street food is food that is cheap and easy to prepare and usually served on a stick. Elote consists of grilled corn on the cob slathered with butter, sour cream, or mayonnaise, and sprinkled with dry cheese, chili powder, and lime or lemon juice.

A legendary street vendor, Timoteo Flor de Nopal, better known as "the Corn Man," peddled elote for more than 30 years in the Lincoln Heights neighborhood of Los Angeles, California. Sometimes lines forming at the Corn Man's small stand would stretch down the block.

19

WORLD'S CORNIEST ATTRACTION!

Mitchell, South Dakota, is home to the world's only Corn Palace! The Corn Palace was built in 1892. It is the chief tourist attraction in Mitchell. Friendly guides offer free tours full of a-maizing facts! Visitors can watch videos on the Corn Palace Story and how corn is grown.

Every year, local artists decorate the Corn Palace's concrete exterior walls with big, colorful murals. The murals are made of thousands of bushels of corn, other grain, and grasses. Also, the city of Mitchell annually hosts the Corn Palace Stampede Rodeo and the Corn Palace Festival.

CORN DOGS FOR ALL!

People in many countries enjoy corn dogs. Australians call corn dogs Dagwood Dogs. In Argentina, corn dogs are made with cheese and sold at train stations. To the people in New Zealand and South Korea, corn dogs are simply hot dogs.

Corn dogs are a fun American snack. They are sold mostly at state or county fairs and festivals. Corn dogs are made of hot dogs on a stick, dipped in corn meal batter and deep fried.

CORN DOGS

Serves 16

INGREDIENTS

1 cup of yellow corn meal
1 cup all-purpose flour
¼ tsp. of salt
⅛ tsp. of black pepper
¼ cup granulated sugar
4 tsp. of baking powder
1 egg
1 cup of milk

1 quart vegetable oil (for frying)
2 16-oz. packages of beef frankfurters (hot dogs)
16 wooden skewers (long pin of wood)

STEPS

1. Combine corn meal, flour, salt, pepper, sugar, and baking powder in a medium bowl. Stir in eggs and milk.
2. Put oil in a deep saucepan and preheat it over medium heat. Stick the wooden skewers into the hot dogs. Roll the hot dogs in the batter until they are fully coated.
3. Fry the corn dogs, 3 at a time, about 3 minutes, until they are lightly browned. Remove the corn dogs from saucepan and place on paper towels to drain off the oil.

LET'S CELEBRATE!

National Corn Dog Day is observed every year on the third Saturday in March.

A TRIP TO THE SUPERMARKET

People eat corn by itself or as an important ingredient in a wide variety of foods. Supermarkets carry hundreds of foods that contain corn or corn products. Some of these foods include breakfast cereal, peanut butter, soups, margarine, syrup, cornstarch, cooking oil, and such snack items as potato chips, cheese puffs, candies, cookies, ice cream, marshmallows, and many other food items.

During our shopping trip, we can also see many kinds of products, other than food, that are made with corn and its byproducts. These nonfood items include aspirin, laundry detergent, dyes, glue, ink, batteries, rust preventatives, shoe polish, soap, construction materials, and paper goods.

CHINA

Corn is eaten in a variety of ways in China. Fresh sweet corn is often mixed into fried rice or moo-shu (stir-fry) dishes in Chinese cooking. Corn is also used in creamy corn chowder, corn soup, corn meal breads, and even ice cream bars.

Although rice is the favorite grain in the south of China, people in the north prefer corn and other grains. Corn on the cob is a popular food mostly sold by street vendors, especially in Beijing.

NOT CORN FED!

Today, China ranks second, behind the United States, in the amount of corn produced in the world each year. But the Chinese eat only a small percentage of the country's corn crop. Most of it is used to feed livestock.

Stir-frying is the traditional method the Chinese use to cook their food, usually with a wok and wok spatula. This distinctive cooking style is popular in Chinese restaurants throughout the world. Although rice and noodles form the base of classic Chinese cooking, such dishes as fried rice and some stir-fry vegetables use corn as a key ingredient.

STIR-FRIED CORN WITH PINE NUTS

Serves about 4

INGREDIENTS

1 tsp. of potato starch
2 tbsp. of chicken stock (liquid flavoring)
¼ cup of pine nuts
2 tsp. of vegetable oil
1 tbsp. of chopped green onion
⅓ cup of carrots cut into small cubes

1 cup of frozen corn
⅓ cup of frozen peas
⅓ cup of cucumber cut into small cubes
¼ tsp. of salt (or salt to taste)
½ tsp. of sugar

STEPS

1. Prep and chop onion, carrots, and cucumber.
2. Using a whisk, beat cornstarch into chicken stock. Set aside.
3. Pour pine nuts into a skillet over medium heat. Stir the pine nuts frequently. When the pine nuts start to brown, turn the heat down to medium low. Cook and stir for another minute, until the pine nuts have turned a light brown. Remove from skillet and place on a plate to cool.
4. Using the same skillet, add oil and turn the heat up to medium high. Stir in chopped green onions a few at a time. Add carrots, peas, and corn. Cook, stirring frequently, until the corn and peas are thawed and the carrots soften to tender. Add cucumber to skillet and season mixture with salt and sugar. Cook for another minute, stirring often, until the cucumber is cooked.
5. Turn the heat off. Whisk the potato starch again and put it in the skillet, mixing well.
6. Taste test for seasoning. If needed, add a little more salt.
7. Stir in toasted pine nuts and mix well.
8. Serve warm.

NOTE: If you want to make this a vegetarian dish, just use water instead of the chicken stock. Also, to minimize prep time, you can buy some of the vegetables already cut up.

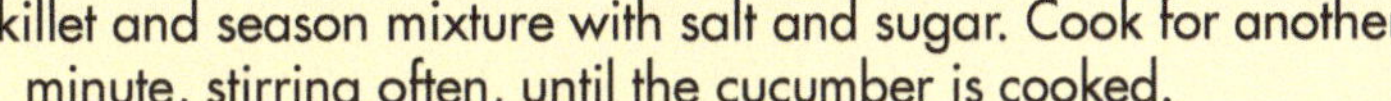

TŌMOROKOSHI IS THE NAME FOR CORN IN JAPAN

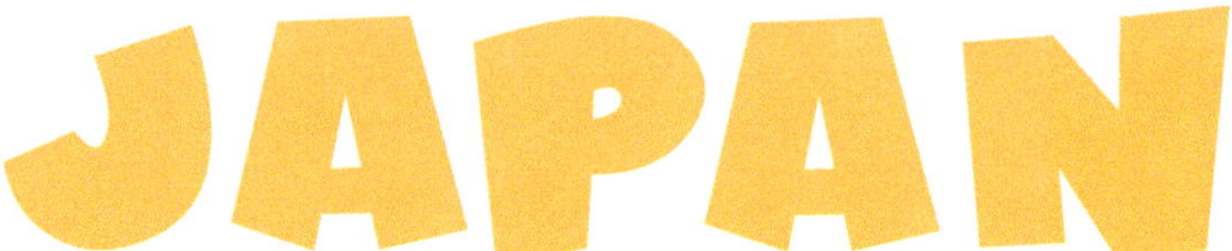

Corn has a long history in Japan. The Portuguese first brought flint corn to Japan from South America in 1579. The Japanese mainly used the grain as livestock feed.

The Japanese began growing sweet corn on a wide scale on Hokkaido, Japan's northern island, in the early 1900's. By the 1950's, sweet corn had become a popular grain in Japan. The most popular sweet corn snack in Hokkaido is corn chocolate. It consists of puffed corns coated with chocolate.

GRILLED CANDY?

In Japan, you can get a Kit Kat candy bar with a grilled corn flavor!

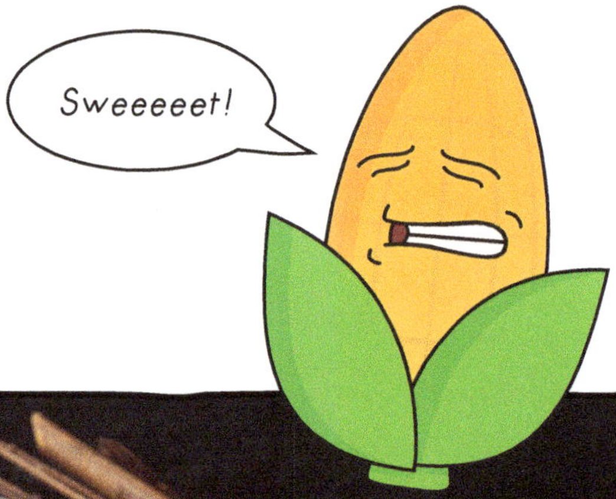

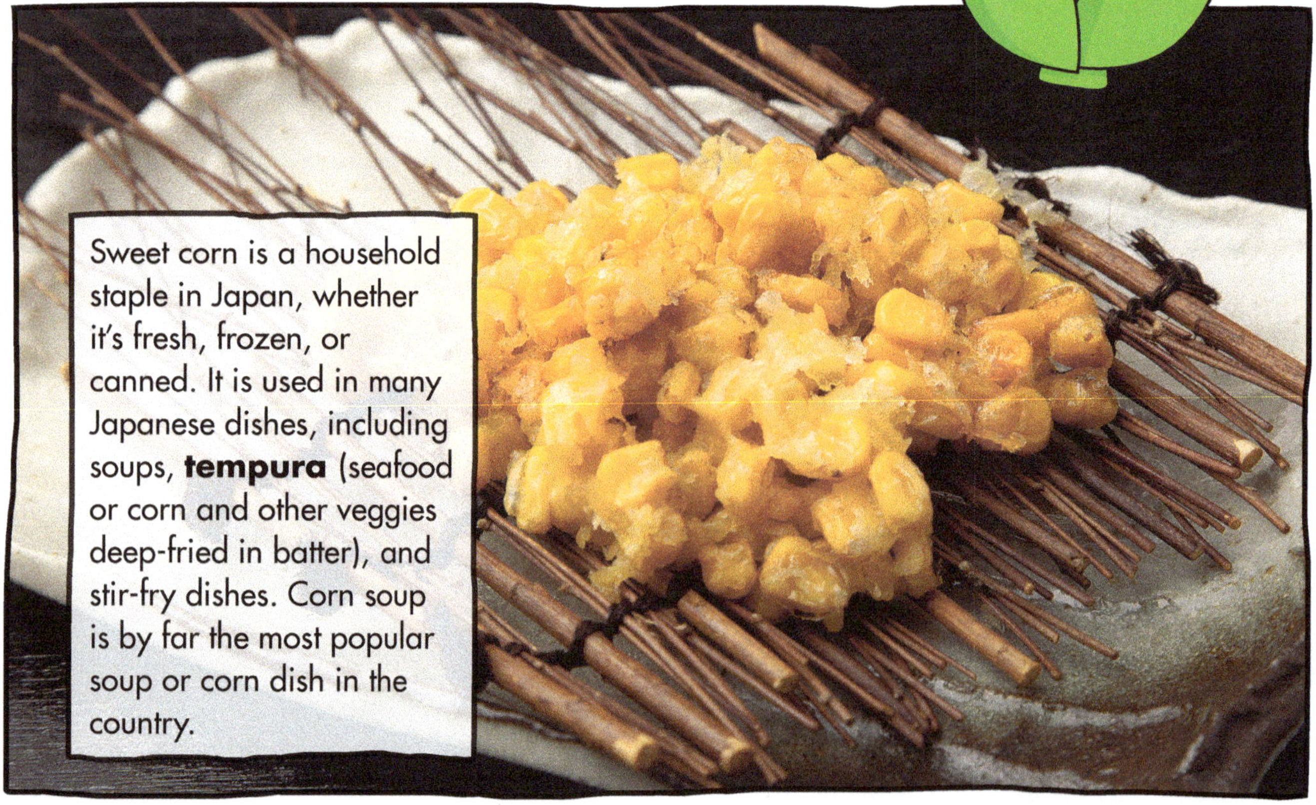

Sweet corn is a household staple in Japan, whether it's fresh, frozen, or canned. It is used in many Japanese dishes, including soups, **tempura** (seafood or corn and other veggies deep-fried in batter), and stir-fry dishes. Corn soup is by far the most popular soup or corn dish in the country.

In the rural village of Oshino, near Mount Fuji, hanging corn cobs out to dry in the outdoor air, either under the eaves or on racks, is a fading winter tradition.

Japan is the world's biggest importer of corn. Most of it comes from the United States.

Say whaaat? The Japanese love to eat their pizza with a corn topping! Corn is also a popular topping for ramen, a Japanese noodle soup.

As in many other countries, corn on the cob is a Japanese favorite at outdoor barbecues and summertime festivals. The Japanese like it boiled, then grilled. While it is cooking, the corn is brushed with miso, or soy sauce, giving it an incredibly pleasant salty, sweet taste.

BRAZIL

Brazilians love to eat corn! They call it milho verde. They use corn to make many dishes and desserts, including the popular dish *cuscuz de milho* or sweet corn meal couscous. It is made of steamed yellow coarse corn meal, coconut flakes, and sweetened condensed milk.

Other Brazilian favorites include corn meal bread, corn meal cake, boiled corn on the cob, corn pudding, popcorn, corn ice cream, and many other dishes. However, unlike in the United States, Brazilians usually make their dishes with field corn (dent or flint corn) instead of sweet corn.

Pamonha is a national dish in Brazil. It is made with a corn masa and wrapped in a fresh corn husk and boiled, like tamales in Mexico. Pamonhas can be savory or sweet and served as a meal, snack, or dessert; hot or cold; and plain or with stuffing.

PAMONHA (CORN MEAL MUSH)

Serves 8

INGREDIENTS

1 cup corn meal

3 cups water

¼ tsp. salt

STEPS

1. Mix together corn meal, one cup of cold water, and salt in a medium saucepan, and stir. Add two cups of boiling water to the cold mixture. Cook over medium heat, stirring frequently, about 5 to 7 minutes, until mixture thickens.
2. If serving as a cereal, spoon mush into bowls and add milk and sugar, if desired. Traditionally, pamonhas are wrapped in cornhusks and boiled, but they can also be fried. If frying, pour mush into a loaf pan and chill completely. Remove from pan and cut into slices. Place slices in a small amount of oil and fry over medium-high heat until both sides are browned. Serve with butter and syrup or honey.

VENEZUELA

The national dish of Venezuela is the **hallaca,** a Venezuelan tamale that has a savory (salty or spicy) and sweet taste. Hallacas are usually prepared only during the Christmas season or given as a Christmas Eve gift. Hallacas consist of corn meal dough filled with a variety of meats and other foods. They are then wrapped in a type of banana leaf, tied up, and steamed. Some historians believe hallacas originated in the 1600's.

The process of making hallacas can be an all-day affair and involve the entire family. Family members form an assembly line and usually take pride in making the hallacas.

A basic part of the Venezuelan diet is a round corn meal cake called an arepa. Arepas can be baked, fried, or grilled. They are eaten daily in the place of bread at most meals. It is usually split open and stuffed with a variety of foods, including meats and cheese.

KINDS OF CORN

There are thousands of varieties of corn. But the six major types of corn are dent corn, flint corn, flour corn, sweet corn, popcorn, and waxy corn. Let's take a look at these different types.

Most farmers use **dent corn** to feed their livestock. They also use **flint corn** as food for livestock. People eat flint corn, too. Flint corn is primarily grown in Central and South America. Many people use flint corn, also called Indian corn, to decorate their homes in the fall.

Flour corn is one of the oldest types of corn.
The kernels of flour corn have many colors,
but most are white or blue. People usually
grow this corn for food just for themselves. It
is mostly grown in parts of the United States,
South America, and South Africa.

MORE KINDS OF CORN

Sweet corn is the sweetest kind of corn. Many people enjoy eating sweet corn right off the cob after the ears have been boiled or roasted. This is known as corn on the cob. The corn kernels can also be removed from the cob, then cooked and eaten. Sweet corn kernels that have been removed from the cob are sold in cans or frozen packages for easy preparation for meals.

DID YOU KNOW that the sticky backing on envelopes is made from waxy corn?

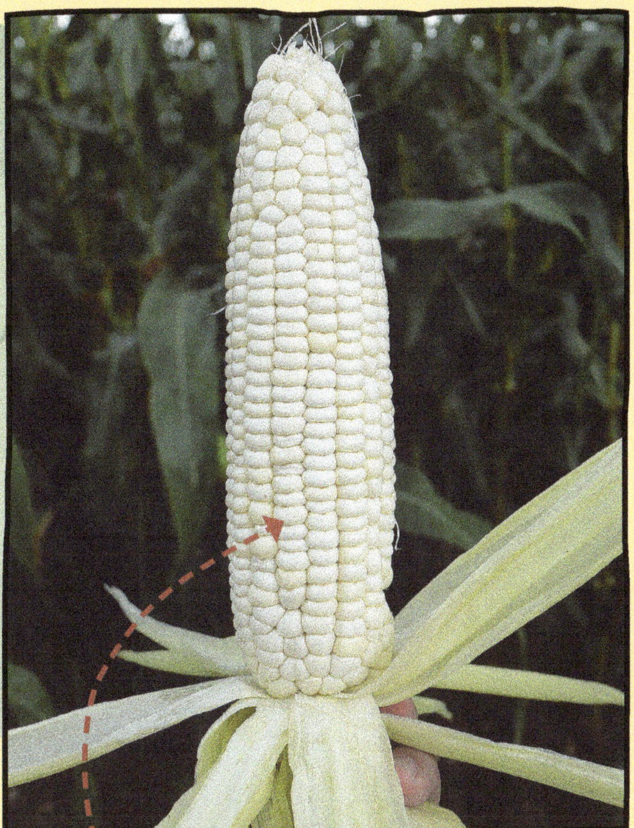

Waxy corn is used to make things stick together. It's also used as a thickener in making instant pudding mixes, gravies and sauces, and glues.

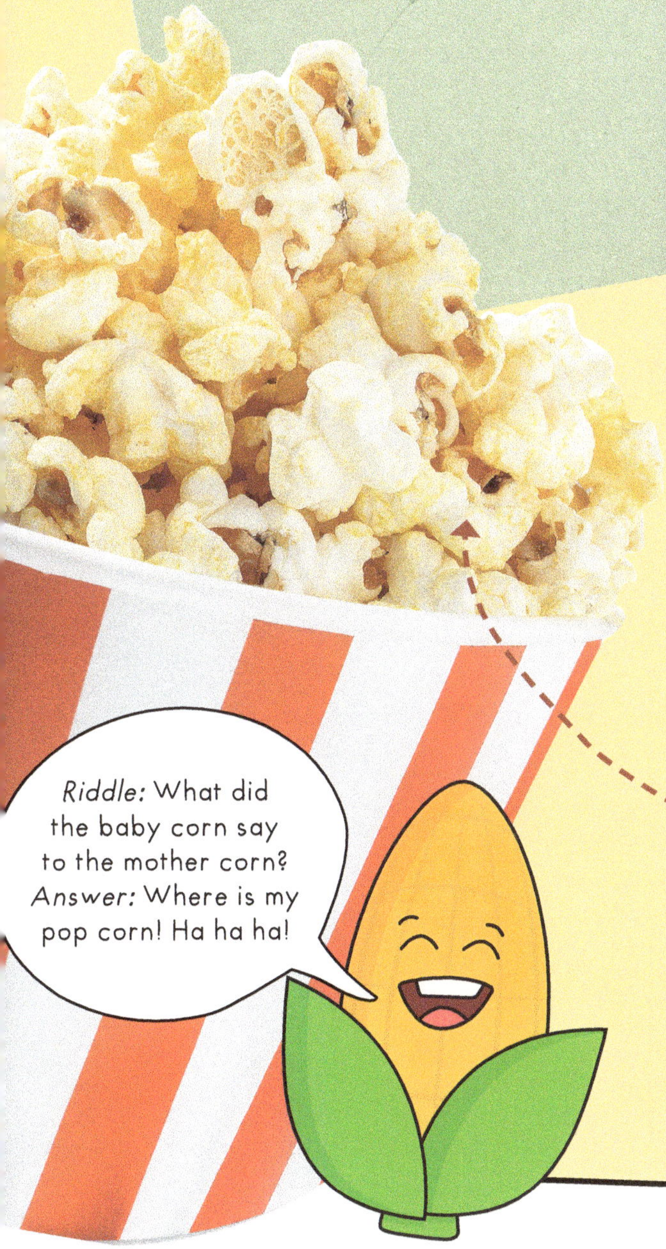

Popcorn is actually a type of flint corn, with very hard kernels. Popcorn is a popular and surprisingly healthy snack food. The kernels in popcorn explode when heated and turn inside-out. The soft center expands and becomes filled with air, making a puffy snack. People usually eat it plain or flavored with salt, butter, caramel, or cheese. Native Americans grew popcorn more than 1,000 years ago. Today, the United States produces most of the popcorn in the world.

CUBA

Corn had been growing in Cuba and throughout the Americas before Columbus arrived. He took some Cuban corn seeds back with him when he returned to Spain in 1493.

Later explorers introduced corn from other parts of the Americas into many areas of the world. By the late 1500's, corn had become a well-established crop in Africa, Asia, southern Europe, and the Middle East.

Many Cuban markets sell corn either ground up or as whole ears. Corn or corn meal is used in a number of Cuban dishes, such as soups *(guiso de maiz)* and tamales. Cuban tamales are much smaller than Mexican tamales and made with corn masa. To make Cuban tamales, the meat is mixed in with the masa, instead of being added as a filling as in Mexican tamales.

TWO ARE BETTER THAN ONE!

Two kinds of corn are grown in Cuba, and neither type is sweet corn. One kind is called *maíz criollo,* or national corn. It is a hard, flint-type and the most common type planted. The other type is called *gibara,* which grows bigger ears.

SOUTH AFRICA

South Africa is one of the leading producers of corn on the continent of Africa. Corn is South Africa's most important grain crop. The South African name for corn is *mealie*.

Corn was introduced to South Africa in the 1600's by the *indigenous* (native) people of northern Africa. They taught the inhabitants of what is now South Africa to grow corn and other vegetables. Corn had originally been brought to the African continent from the Americas by the Portuguese.

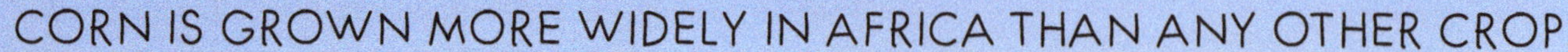

The basic food for many South Africans is corn (mealies). It's usually cooked into a soft porridge called pap. Pap is made up of ground corn and is a lot like American grits. For a complete meal, it is usually served hot or cold with savory meat or vegetable stew.

MEALIE SOUP (CORN SOUP)

Serves 6

INGREDIENTS

4 tbsp. butter
1 cup onions, finely chopped
2 tomatoes, chopped
2 cups whole kernel sweet corn, drained
2 cups cream style sweet corn

1 12-oz. can evaporated milk
3 cups chicken broth (about 1½ cans)
1 tbsp. salt
1 tsp. black pepper

STEPS

1. Melt butter in large saucepan over medium heat.
2. Stir in the onions and sauté for 5 minutes.
3. Add the tomatoes and cook for a few minutes.
4. Add the corn, milk, chicken broth, salt, and pepper. Simmer for 15 minutes.
5. Serve hot, with or without crackers.

PHILIPPINES

Filipino farmers produce most of the food for the entire population in the Philippines. Corn is the second most important food crop, after rice. One out of five Filipinos eats corn as a staple food. But the Filipino population eats only about 21 percent of the country's corn. Most of the rest is used for feed for livestock and poultry.

DID YOU KNOW that fresh corn on the cob loses nearly half of its sugar content after being stored at room temperature for six hours? The sugar changes to starch.

WHITE OR YELLOW?

White corn is the most popular type of corn in the Philippines. With its small sweet kernels, it is usually eaten roasted or boiled. Yellow corn is the other type of corn grown. It is larger than white corn and is grown mostly as feed corn. Yellow corn can also be eaten, but it is very dry and hard.

DID YOU KNOW that
boiled sweet corn is a
popular street food snack
throughout the Philippines?
It is usually seasoned with
salt and butter and served
on the cob or just the
kernels in a cup, mixed with
cheese powder and butter.

CORN'S USES!

Corn is one of the world's most important crops. There are more than 3,500 uses for corn products.

Corn is very valuable as a food. It is rich in fats, proteins, and other things people need to stay healthy. Corn is one of the chief sources of energy in people's diet. We need energy for everything we do, such as walking, talking, working, playing, reading, and even thinking and breathing.

Corn kernels—that is, the grain or seeds— can simply be cooked and eaten. The kernels can also be used in making such things as salad dressing, baked goods, baby food, and many other food items.

Corn is a major feed for farm animals. Farmers in many countries use large quantities of corn to feed livestock. Food for pets often contains corn.

About half of the corn harvested in the United States each year becomes feed for hogs, cattle, sheep, and poultry. Farm animals also eat the stalk and other parts of the corn plant. People indirectly eat the corn fed to livestock in the form of meat, eggs, and dairy products.

STONE EARS!

Ears of corn are carved into the stone columns in the United States Capitol building.

MORE THINGS YOU CAN DO WITH CORN!

Many plastic products, including some grocery bags, are made from corn. It's called *corn plastic,* and it's recyclable and biodegradable! That means it can be used again and it breaks down naturally in the environment, unlike traditional oil-based plastic bags, which are being banned in some countries. Corn plastics are also used in making some plastic eating utensils, coffee mugs, sports and water bottles, and even T-shirts!

Corn syrup is one of the main ingredients in cough drops, as well as many hard candies and lollipops, providing that flavorful sweetness. It is also used to give some types of candies, such as caramels, jellies, and marshmallows, a chewy texture. Corn syrup is beneficial for producers of cough drops to use because it's cheaper than white sugar.

Corn has many industrial uses as well. Corn is used to make such products as paints and plastics, ceramics, cosmetics, explosives, drugs, paper goods, soap, nail polish, fabrics, construction materials, and hundreds of other items.

Corn products help the colorful crayons that children play with keep their shape. Corn products also help the paper labels stick to the crayons.

GLOSSARY

atole *(ah TOH lay)* A popular hot, thick Mexican beverage made from corn; a mush or gruel made of the meal of Indian corn in Spanish-American countries.

balché *(bahl CHAY)* A fermented drink of the Maya, made from corn and spiced with honey and the bark of the balché tree.

burrito *(bur REE toh)* A large tortilla filled with cheese, beans, vegetables, rice, and hot sauce.

elote *(ay LOH tay)* Corn on the cob with cheese; a street food.

enchilada *(EHN chih LAH duh)* Rolled-up tortillas filled with chopped meat or cheese and covered with red chili sauce.

grits *(grihts)* An American dish of coarsely ground corn boiled in milk or water and eaten traditionally as a breakfast food.

hallaca *(ah YAH kuh)* A Venezuelan Christmas dish; a tamale made of corn meal dough filled with meats and other foods and wrapped in a type of banana leaf, tied up, and steamed.

hush-puppy A small ball of corn meal deep fried in fat, usually served as a side dish.

masa harina *(MAH sah ah REEN ah)* A type of corn flour used to make tortillas, tamales, and other Mexican dishes.

polenta *(poh LEHN tuh)* A thick porridge made of corn meal, commonly eaten in Italy.

pozole *(poh SOH lay)* A Mexican soup made with hominy, meat, and other ingredients.

quesadilla *(kays uh DEE yuh)* A tortilla folded over a simple filling, often containing cheese, and then fried.

taco *(TAH koh)* A fried tortilla filled with meat, cheese, beans, tomatoes, lettuce, and sauce.

tamale *(tuh MAH lee)* A Mexican food made of corn meal and ground meat, seasoned with red peppers, wrapped in cornhusks, and roasted or steamed.

tempura *(tehm PUR uh)* A Japanese dish of seafood or vegetables deep-fried in batter.

teosinte *(tay oh SEEN tay)* A tall grass related to corn, native to Mexico and Central America.

tōmorokoshi *(TOH moh roh koh shee)* Japanese name for corn.

tortilla *(tawr TEE yuh)* A thin, round flatbread made from corn meal or flour.

tostada *(taws TAH thah)* A tortilla fried in deep fat until it becomes crisp and served flat with meat, cheese, beans, lettuce, and onions.

HELPFUL HINTS

When working in the kitchen with food, keep these helpful hints in mind to make sure your work goes smoothly and safely. Then enjoy the tasty treats you make!

- **Wash your hands** before you begin food preparation and after you've touched raw eggs or meat.
- Thoroughly **wash fruits and vegetables.**
- **Use oven mitts** when handling hot pots, pans, or trays.
- **Have an adult help** when working with knives and hot stoves or ovens.

INDEX

World Book, Inc.
180 North LaSalle Street
Suite 900
Chicago, Illinois 60601
USA

For information about other "Taste the World!" titles, as well as other World Book print and digital publications, please go to www.worldbook.com.

For information about other World Book publications, call 1-800-WORLDBK (967-5325).

For information about sales to schools and libraries, call 1-800-975-3250 (United States) or 1-800-837-5365 (Canada).

Library of Congress Cataloging-in-Publication Data

Title: Corn
Description: Chicago, Illinois: World Book Inc., [2020] | Series: Taste the world! | Includes index.
Identifiers: LCCN 2019037376 | ISBN 9780716628606 (hardcover)
Subjects: LCSH: Cooking (Corn)--Juvenile literature. | Corn--History--Juvenile literature. | International cooking--Juvenile literature.
Classification: LCC TX809.M2 C65 2020 | DDC 641.6/315--dc23
LC record available at https://lccn.loc.gov/2019037376

Taste the World!
ISBN: 978-0-7166-2858-3 (set, hc.)

Corn
ISBN: 978-0-7166-4762-1

Also available as:
ISBN: 978-0-7166-2868-2 (e-book)

2nd printing July 2020

STAFF

Editorial

Writer: Mellonee Carrigan

Manager, New Product Development
Nick Kilzer

Proofreader: Nathalie Strassheim

Manager, Contracts and Compliance
(Rights and Permissions): Loranne K. Shields

Manager, Indexing Services
David Pofelski

Digital

Director, Digital Product Development
Erika Meller

Digital Product Manager
Jonathan Wills

Graphics and Design

Coordinator, Design Development
and Production
Brenda Tropinski

Senior Visual Communications Designer
Melanie Bender

Media Editor: Rosalia Bledsoe

Senior Web Designer/Digital Media Developer
Matt Carrington

Manufacturing/Production

Manufacturing Manager: Anne Fritzinger

Production Specialist: Curley Hunter

ACKNOWLEDGMENTS

Cover   © Kzww/Shutterstock; © Slavica Stajic, Shutterstock
Character artwork by Matthew Carrington
   2-3   Public Domain (Florentine Codex); © Shutterstock
   4-9   © Shutterstock
   10-11   © Fotokostic/Shutterstock; © Vainillaychile/Shutterstock; Nicolle Rager Fuller, National Science Foundation; *Figurine Whistle of a Maize God Seated on a Personified Mountain* (AD 600-900), Ceramic by Northern Guatemala or Southeastern Mexico, Maya; Los Angeles County Museum of Art
   12-13   © AGCuesta/Shutterstock; © Kzww/Shutterstock; Public Domain (Florentine Codex); © BW Folsom/Shutterstock
   14-15   © Shutterstock
   16-17   © Hillary Fox, iStockphoto; Library of Congress; *The First Thanksgiving, 1621* (1912-1915), oil on canvas by Jean Leon Gerome Ferris; Library of Congress; © James Brey, iStockphoto
   18-25   © Shutterstock
   24-25   © Drevs/Shutterstock; © Misandao/iStockphoto
   26-37   © Shutterstock
   38-39   © Cameron Watson, Shutterstock; © Maks Narodenko, Shutterstock; © Alexander Van Berge, StockFood/age fotostock
   40-41   © Nataly Studio/Shutterstock; © Art Phaneuf, Alamy Images
   42-45   © Shutterstock